Child's Guide to First Holy Communion

BY ELIZABETH FICOCELLI

ILLUSTRATIONS BY ANNE CATHARINE BLAKE

PAULIST PRESS
New York/Mahwah, N.J.

Caseside design by Lynn Else
Caseside illustrations by Anne Catharine Blake

ISBN: 0-8091-6708-5

Published by Paulist Press
997 Macarthur Boulevard
Mahwah, New Jersey 07430

www.paulistpress.com

Printed and bound in Mexico

To my husband, Mark,
who has blessed my life with hope, love,
and the gift of the Catholic faith.

E. F.

For Eric Andrew Blake

A. C. B.

My name is _Taryn_

I celebrated my First Holy Communion on

_____

Helping me celebrate were

_____

_____

_____

Hi! My name is Justin. This is where I go to church.

Today is a very special day for me. I've been preparing for it for a long time. Today I am celebrating my *First Holy Communion*. This means I am going to invite Jesus into my heart in a new and wonderful way.

Come with me, the celebration is about to begin!

"Hi, Olivia!" I say to my classmate. "I like your dress."
"Thanks, Justin. You look nice, too."

Today is a good day to wear special clothes if you have them. But if you don't have them, it doesn't matter. More important than how we look on the outside is how we *feel* on the *inside* — happy and ready to receive Jesus!

What does feeling special on the inside mean?

As we walk in, I smile at everyone. I see moms and dads, brothers and sisters, aunts and uncles, grandmas and grandpas, cousins and friends. We sing a song about how all the people in church belong to one family in Jesus. That's a big family! I sing extra loud.

Can you find Justin's family? Olivia's?
Who goes to church with *you*?

Mass begins just like it always does. My family brings me to Mass every Sunday to learn about Jesus, so I feel right at home in church. Look, there's Father Mario. He leads us in prayer. Together, we ask God to forgive our sins.

What is the name of your parish? Your parish priest?

Now it's time to sit and listen to the word of God. Today's readings are all about Holy Communion. My friend, Ramón, is going to read a letter from Saint Paul.

"...the Lord Jesus, on the night he was handed over, took bread...."

I know this story. It's about the very first *Communion*. *Communion* means to join together. Jesus, on the night before he died on the cross for us, had a *Last Supper* with his good friends, the *Apostles*. Jesus wanted his friends to know how much he loved them. He wanted them to know that he would always be with them. So Jesus gave himself in a very special way through bread and wine — a way that would join him to his friends forever.

"Take and eat. This is my body.
Take and drink. This is my blood.
Do this in memory of me."

The next story we hear in church today is read by Father Mario. It is the Gospel, the good news of Jesus. We stand for this important reading.

"...taking the five loaves and the two fish, and looking up to heaven, he said the blessing over them...."

I know this story, too. It's about how Jesus fed 5,000 people. He took two fish and five loaves of bread and said a special blessing. Then he told his Apostles to feed the people. There was plenty for everyone! It was a miracle. At Mass, the same kind of miracle happens when Jesus tells his priests to feed the people. This time, Jesus feeds us with his body and blood during Holy Communion.

**Imagine you are one of those people being fed by Jesus.
How do you feel?**

After the Gospel is read, Father Mario talks to us. He says that our First Holy Communion is a good reason to dress up. It's fine to have a party on this day with cake and gifts, but the best gift we will ever receive is the gift of Jesus. Father Mario reminds us how Jesus is the Bread of Life. Jesus promised that no one who comes to him will ever be hungry. Now we, too, are ready to be fed.

Next we sing a song of preparation.

While we sing, Darryl and Theresa carry bread and wine up to Father Mario. Bread and wine are gifts from the earth which God created. Father Mario places them on the altar.

We give thanks to God for all his gifts. We thank him for the bread and wine. We thank him for his love. Most of all, we thank him for giving us his son, Jesus.

Another word for Communion is *Eucharist. Eucharist* means to give thanks.

There is so much to be thankful for.
Blessed be God forever!

What are you thankful for?

Father Mario holds up the *host*, a flat white bread in the shape of a circle. He holds it high so we can all see it. He says the same words Jesus said to his friends at the Last Supper. *"Take this, all of you, and eat. This is my body given up for you."*

I bow my head quietly. I know Jesus is here with us now.

Then Father Mario holds up
the *chalice,* the cup of wine. This too he
holds high so we can see it. *"Take this,
all of you, and drink. This is the blood of
the new and everlasting covenant. Do this
in memory of me."*

I bow my head again.

Even though I still see bread and wine, I know they have become the body and blood of Jesus. This is called the *consecration*. Now Jesus is really and truly present. In a way that we don't fully understand, the bread and wine are changed forever. So are the people who receive Communion.

When I receive Jesus today, I will be joined to him in a special way, just like the Apostles were at the Last Supper. But I'm not the only one. All of the people who receive Communion today will also be joined to Jesus and to each other.

To show our communion with one another, we pray for the church and for people who have died. We pray *The Lord's Prayer*. And then we give each other the *Sign of Peace*.

Practice giving the Sign of Peace in class or at home.

Finally, it's time to receive our First Holy Communion. One by one, with our moms and dads behind us, we walk up to Father Mario. I see Olivia and her family ahead of me, walking toward the altar.

In class we learned that the host can be a thin white circle. It can be brown and thick like a cracker. It can even be pointy, if it is broken off from a bigger piece.

We practiced receiving the host. First we cupped our hands, one beneath the other, and were given a host. Then we picked it up gently. We learned we should put the host in our mouths at once, carefully, while we are still standing at the altar. We learned never to walk away while the host is in our hands.

We also practiced taking a small sip of wine from a cup. It tasted kind of funny. We learned not to make faces but to show respect, because at Mass it is really Jesus we are receiving.

We learned never to be afraid to come to Jesus. No one is perfect, and we all make mistakes. God loves us anyway and forgives us if we ask. We were taught a special prayer to ask for forgiveness. I say it to myself now:

My God, I am sorry for my sins with all my heart. In choosing to do wrong and failing to do good, I have sinned against you whom I should love above all things. I firmly intend, with your help, to do penance, to sin no more, and to avoid whatever leads me to sin.

Can you think of a time when you did something that wasn't nice? Ask God to forgive you now.

Now, it's *my* turn. My heart is pounding hard. I walk up to Father Mario. He smiles at me. "The body of Christ, Justin," he says.

"*Amen,*" I answer. That means, "I agree." I put my hands out carefully, and Father Mario places the small white host in my hand. I put it in my mouth. I take a sip from the cup. I know Jesus is very near to me now.

When I sit down at my seat, I close my eyes and think about Jesus sitting next to me, with his arms around me. I feel very close to him. I know Jesus loves me and wants to be with me. I know he wants me to bring his love to everyone I meet.

My mom and dad smile at me. They are very proud. I feel proud, too.

To celebrate Jesus with us, we sing another song about being God's people. My family smiles and waves to me as I walk out. Grandma takes a picture of me.

Outside, there's lots of laughing and hugging. And more pictures! My uncle hands me a gift. It's a First Holy Communion pin. I remember what Father Mario said about Jesus being my greatest gift.

This has been a happy day. But you want to know the best part? The next time I go to Mass, and every time after that, I get to receive Jesus all over again! He will be with me this special way for the rest of my life.

I can hardly wait for my *second* Holy Communion!